# SCOOBY-DOO
## AND THE BURIED CITY OF POMPEII

# THE GHASTLY GUIDE

BY MARK WEAKLAND

Consultant: Jesse Weiner, PhD
Assistant Professor of Classics
Hamilton College

CAPSTONE PRESS
a capstone imprint

Scooby-Doo and the gang were on vacation in Italy. They were about to start a sightseeing tour of the famous ruins of Pompeii.

Shaggy sighed happily. "Like, it feels good to take a break from solving mysteries."

Velma nodded. "I want to see everything here. This place is so well preserved — the streets, the houses, the . . ."

### SCOOBY FACT

The city of Pompeii covers 150 acres. It is one of the world's largest excavated archeological sites.

A long, low moan drifted out from behind an ancient wall. "Oooow!"

"So much for our vacation," exclaimed Fred. "We have a mystery on our hands!"

"A Roman ghost? Like, no way," said Shaggy, folding his arms. "I'm here on vacation."

"Reah, racation," said Scooby.

"Come on, you two," said Fred. "We can't turn our backs on a mystery. Besides, we can still sightsee."

"Like, count us out," said Shaggy.

"I guess we're solving a mystery," said Shaggy as he munched on his snack.

The gang walked toward the moaning sound. Ahead were the ancient columns of Pompeii. Beyond the city loomed an enormous volcano.

"That's Mount Vesuvius," said Fred, pointing up. "It's one of the most dangerous volcanoes in the world."

"You're right, Freddy," said Daphne. "The volcano is only 5 miles away from Pompeii, and it's still active."

"Active?" Shaggy's eyes grew large. "Like with steam and lava and explosions?"

"Roh no!" said Scooby, covering his eyes.

"Don't worry, Shaggy and Scooby," said Velma. "We're safe here."

### SCOOBY FACT

Mount Vesuvius is the only active volcano on Europe's mainland. The last major eruption was in 1944.

Velma pulled a tablet from her bag and showed the gang what the city of Pompeii looked like centuries ago.

"Almost 2,000 years ago, Pompeii was a flourishing city. The weather was warm and sunny. The landscape was beautiful," said Velma, pointing to a painting. "More than 20,000 people lived in Pompeii. Many of Rome's most important citizens visited there."

Velma enlarged a painting of a home in the ancient city. "Elegant houses lined the paved streets. There were small businesses and factories. Townspeople, visitors, and slaves bustled in and out of shops that sold food, clothes, and jewelry. There were taverns, cafes, theaters, and bathhouses. There was also an amphitheater."

As the gang looked over Velma's shoulders, a moaning sound echoed in the distance. "Ooooww!"

"It's coming from the amphitheater!" cried Daphne. "This way!"

Daphne took off toward the amphitheater as the others followed closely behind. Inside, Daphne saw a flash of white in the stands. Then it disappeared.

"I saw something over there! Let's look around."

"There's nothing here," cried Fred. "It looks like it got away." Shaggy stared up at the ruins of the giant structure. "Like, wow. Look at this place!"

"This is the world's oldest standing Roman amphitheater," said Velma. "Before it was destroyed, people came here from all over to watch gladiator battles and other Roman games. There was a cloth roof that protected spectators from the sun, wind, and rain."

### SCOOBY FACT

The amphitheater at Pompeii is the earliest known permanent amphitheater in Italy. It could have held as many as 20,000 people.

11

The gang walked out of the amphitheater. "Like, what happened to this city?" asked Shaggy. "How was it destroyed?"

Velma held up her tablet and read. "On August 24, 79 A.D., Mount Vesuvius violently erupted. First came a blast of ash and rock. A column of smoke, ash, and steam rose so high that people hundreds of miles away saw it."

Scooby gulped and stared up at the volcano as Velma continued.

"As the blast cooled, ash rained down on the city. Many townspeople fled, but others stayed. As the day went on, the conditions grew worse. More ash fell, causing buildings to collapse."

"The next day a cloud of superheated poisonous gas escaped from the volcano and covered the city," added Fred.

## SCOOBY FACT

The nearby town of Herculaneum was also destroyed when Mount Vesuvius erupted.

"You're right, Fred," said Velma. "By the end more than 1,500 people were killed, and Pompeii had disappeared under 13 to 20 feet of ash. The town was abandoned for centuries."

The gang continued searching for the ghost, walking up one street and down the next. Velma led them past excavated houses on a hillside.

As they looked, Velma told the gang more about the city's history.

In 1748 a group of explorers came to Pompeii looking for artifacts. They dug through the ash. Eventually they discovered an entire town, almost exactly like it was hundreds of years before.

How could the town look the same?

I'll show you. Follow me.

Velma lead the gang into one of the many thermopolia in Pompeii. Archeologists believe shops like this sold food and other goods.

"The ash from the volcano's eruption came down hard and fast. It completely covered Pompeii, freezing it in time," explained Velma. "When Pompeii was discovered, its streets and buildings were still intact within the ash."

"That's incredible!" said Daphne, looking at one of the clay containers.

"Explorers found hundreds of these clay containers still sitting in a granary," said Velma. "Beautiful statues and intricate paintings were still in homes. A bakery even had a loaf of bread in its oven!"

Fred wiped his forehead. "Wow, it's hot out here. And there's no sign of the moaning ghost."

"Like, let's find a shady spot," said Shaggy.

The gang moved closer to one of the walls to shade themselves from the sun.

"Rut's rat?" asked Scooby, pointing to a wall.

"Ancient Romans scrawled graffiti on the walls of houses, shops, and taverns to communicate messages," said Daphne. "They drew pictures, wrote funny sayings and love notes, and campaigned for people running in elections."

Shaggy peered at the graffiti. "I can't read a word of this." "That's because it's written in Latin," said Velma. "I'll translate." Velma approached the wall for a closer look. "These two say 'Rufus loves Cornelia' and 'Staphylus was here.' This one says 'Vote for Cornelius.'"

The gang continued their search. Next they entered an ancient home covered with beautiful artwork on the walls and floors.

"This is the House of the Tragic Poet. Discovered in 1824, this home shows how people lived in Pompeii."

Velma stared at the black and white mosaic on the floor.

"This says "CAVE CANEM." That means beware of the dog!"

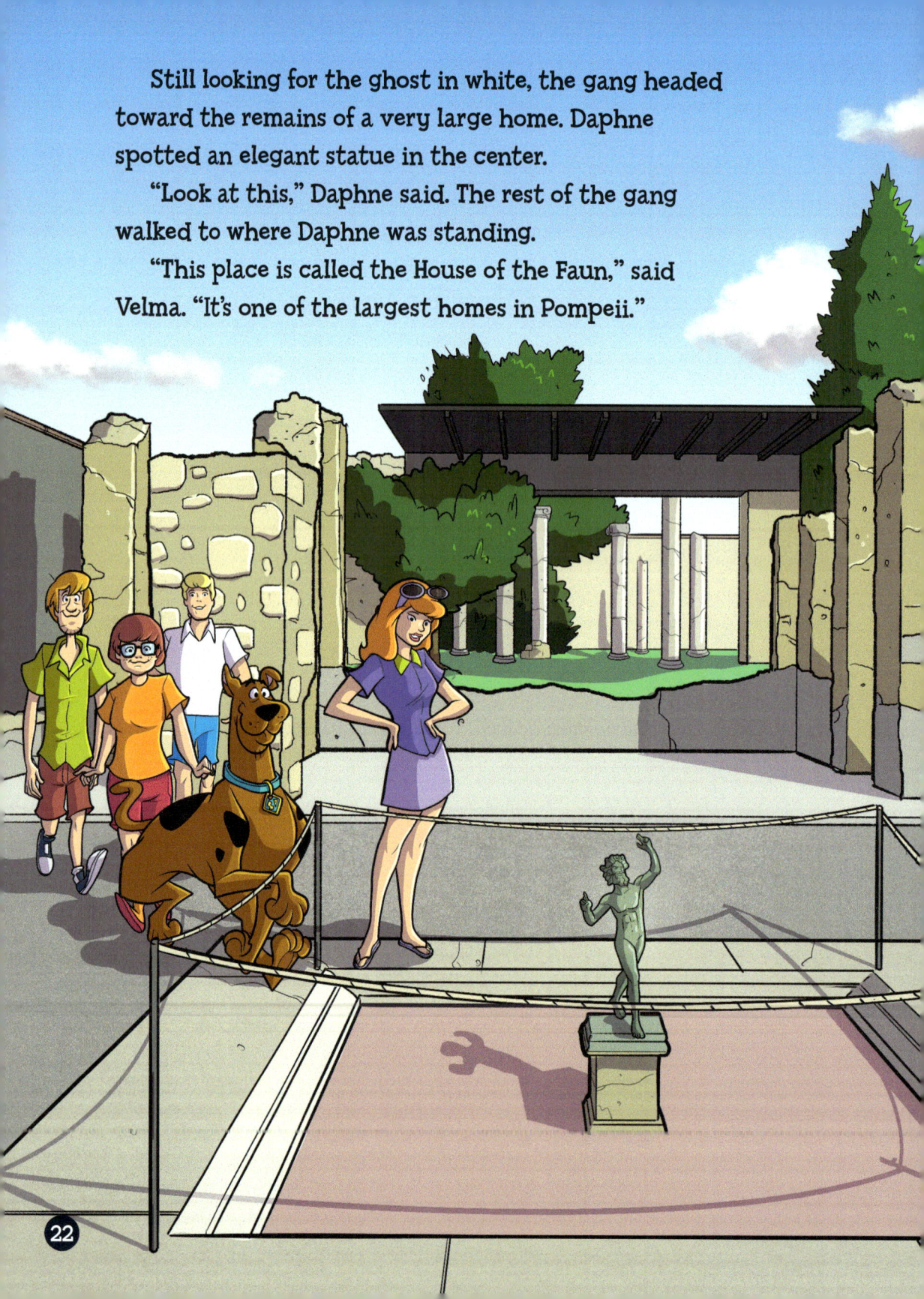

Still looking for the ghost in white, the gang headed toward the remains of a very large home. Daphne spotted an elegant statue in the center.

"Look at this," Daphne said. The rest of the gang walked to where Daphne was standing.

"This place is called the House of the Faun," said Velma. "It's one of the largest homes in Pompeii."

The house is named for this statue of a dancing faun. It's in the center of what used to be the house's main hall. Whoever lived here was very wealthy.

The gang continued their investigation. Along a wall under a tree, they came upon an eerie sight — the Garden of Fugitives. Plaster casts of people killed at Pompeii lay twisted on the ground.

"What is this place?" said Daphne, looking at the casts.

"These are plaster molds of people who died when Mount Vesuvius erupted," said Velma. "When archeologists uncovered this area, they found that the bodies had made holes in the ash. Archeologists poured plaster into the holes. When the ash was removed, the plaster casts revealed what the victims looked like when they died."

Suddenly the ghostly figure in white sprinted by.

Ooow! Ow, ow!

After it!

Rounding a corner, the gang saw a bearded man sitting in the shade. He was dressed in flowing white robes.

The man groaned. "Owww!"

"Hey, you're no ghost," said Daphne.

"Ghost? Hardly," said the man. "I'm a tour guide."

"Why are you dressed like that?" asked Fred, pointing to the guide's robes.

"This is my costume," said the guide. "I'm dressed like an ancient Roman high priest. I thought it would entertain the tourists."

"Then why pretend to be a ghost?" asked Shaggy. "Why all the moaning and running?"

The guide rubbed his feet. "I'm not pretending to be anything. My sandal straps broke, so I had to walk around in my bare feet. These Pompeii paving stones are hot!"

"Well gang, it looks like we've solved another mystery. Now let's get back to our vacation!"

"Like, you don't have to tell us twice!"

"Rou raid it, Raggy!"

# SCOOBY SNACK-SIZED FACTS

- Starting at age 7, children from wealthy Pompeiian families went to school. Children from poor families were sent to work.

- The most common foods in Pompeii were beans, lentils, and bread. There were also olives, grapes, meat, and fish.

- Mount Vesuvius is 4,202 feet (1,281 meters) high. Scientists estimate it has erupted more than 50 times in the past 17,000 years.

- The eruption that destroyed Pompeii happened a day after a religious festival called Vulcanalia. The festival celebrated Vulcan, the Roman god of fire.

- Today more than 3 million people live close to Mount Vesuvius. More people live close to this dangerous volcano than any other active volcano in the world.

# Glossary

**amphitheater** (AM-fi-thee-uh-tur)—a large, open-air building with rows of seats in a high circle around the building; in ancient Roman times, amphitheaters were used for public entertainment, such as gladiator and animal fights

**ancient** (AYN-shunt)—from a long time ago

**archeologist** (ar-kee-AH-luh-jist)—a scientist who learns about people in the past by digging up old buildings and objects and carefully examining them

**artifact** (ART-uh-fakt)—an object made or changed by human beings, especially a tool or weapon used in the past

**erupt** (i-RUHPT)—to burst suddenly with great force

**excavate** (EK-skuh-vate)—to dig in the earth, either to put up a building or to search for ancient remains

**graffiti** (gruh-FEE-tee)—pictures drawn or words written on the walls of buildings or other surfaces

**granary** (GRAN-uh-ree)—a building for storing grain

**mosaic** (moh-ZAY-ik)—a pattern or picture made up of small pieces of colored stone, tile, or glass

## READ MORE

**O'Connor, Jim.** *What Was Pompeii?* What Was …? New York: Crosset & Dunlap, 2014.

**O'Shei, Tim.** *Secrets of Pompeii: Buried City of Ancient Rome.* Archeological Mysteries. North Mankato, Minn.: Capstone Press, 2015.

**Yomtov, Nelson.** *Peril in Pompeii: Nickolas Flux and the Eruption of Mount Vesuvius.* Nickolas Flux History Chronicles. North Mankato, Minn.: 2015.

## INTERNET SITES

Use FactHound to find Internet sites related to this book.

Visit www.facthound.com

Just type in 9781515775126 and go.

**Super-cool stuff!** Check out projects, games and lots more at www.capstonekids.com

# INDEX

amphitheaters, 9, 10—11, 12
ashes, 12, 13, 15, 16, 25

casts, 24, 25

foods, 9, 16, 17, 28

Garden of the Fugitives, 24—25
gladiators, 11
graffiti, 18, 19
granaries, 17

Herculaneum, 13
high priests, 26
House of the Faun, 22—23
House of the Tragic Poet, 20—21

Italy, 2, 11

mosaics, 21
Mount Vesuvius, 6, 7, 12, 13, 16, 25, 28

thermopolia, 16

Vulcanalia, 28

Published in 2018 by Capstone Press, a Capstone Imprint
1710 Roe Crest Drive
North Mankato, Minnesota 56003
www.mycapstone.com

Copyright © 2018 Hanna-Barbera. SCOOBY-DOO and all related characters and elements are trademarks of and © Hanna-Barbera. WB SHIELD: ™ & © Warner Bros. Entertainment Inc. (s18)
CAPS39504

All rights reserved. No part of this publication may be reproduced in whole or in part, or stored in a retrieval system, or transmitted in any form or by any means, electronic, mechanical, photocopying, recording, or otherwise, without written permission of the publisher.

**Library of Congress Cataloging-in-Publication Data**
Names: Weakland, Mark, author.
Title: Scooby-Doo! and the buried city of Pompeii : the ghastly guide / by Mark Weakland.
Description: North Mankato, Minnesota : Capstone Press, 2018. | Series: Scooby-Doo!: Unearthing ancient civilizations with Scooby-Doo!

Identifiers: LCCN 2017034026 (print) | LCCN 2017035880 (ebook) | ISBN 9781515775201 (eBook PDF) | ISBN 9781515775126 (library binding) | ISBN 9781515775164 (paperback)
Subjects: LCSH: Pompeii (Extinct city)—Juvenile literature. | Vesuvius (Italy)—Eruption, 79—Juvenile literature.
Classification: LCC DG70.P7 (ebook) | LCC DG70.P7 W397 2018 (print) |
DDC 937/.72568—dc23
LC record available at https://lccn.loc.gov/2017034026

**Editorial Credits:**
Editor: Michelle Hasselius
Designer: Ted Williams
Art Director: Nathan Gassman
Production Specialist: Laura Manthe

**Design Elements:**
Shutterstock/natashasha

The illustrations in this book were created traditionally, with digital coloring.

## TITLES IN THIS SET

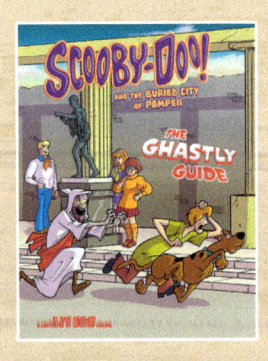

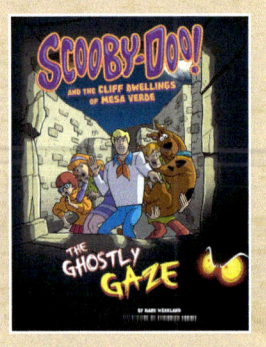

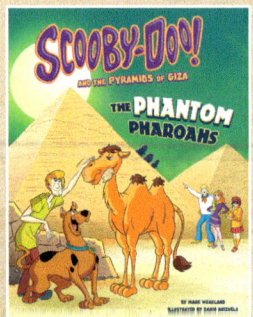

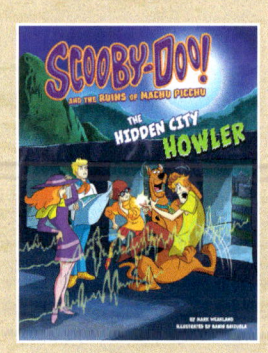

Printed in the United States of America.
2593